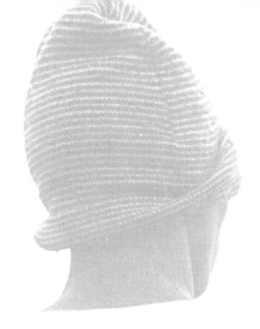

THE
CRISIS IN
SOUTH AFRICA

Ieuan Griffiths

ROURKE ENTERPRISES INC.
Vero Beach, Florida 32964

Library of Congress Cataloging-in-Publication Data

Griffiths, Ieuan Ll.
  The crisis in South Africa.
  Bibliography: p.
  Includes index.
  1. Apartheid—South Africa.   2. South Africa—
Ethnic relations.   I. Title.
DT763.G695   1989   305.8′00968   88-3235
ISBN 0-86592-035-4

Text © 1988 Rourke Enterprises Inc.
PO Box 3328, Vero Beach, Florida, 32964

Manufactured in England

Contents

1
Sharpeville

"History, I believe, will recognize that Sharpeville marked a watershed in South African affairs."

Ambrose Reeves, Bishop of Johannesburg

On March 21, 1960 at Sharpeville Location outside the town of Vereeniging in the southern Transvaal, South Africa, 69 Black Africans were shot dead and 186 were wounded by the South African Police. Of the bullet wounds that could be classified, 30 had entered the killed or wounded persons from the front, and 155 from the back.

A crowd of 5,000 Black people had gathered at Sharpeville Police Station to offer themselves for arrest as part of a peaceful Pan Africanist Congress (PAC) protest against the pass laws. The demonstrators were not carrying their pass books, as was required by these laws. The crowd, comprising unarmed men, women and children, was noisy and excitable but not hostile. The massacre was sparked off by two White policemen who fired shots into the crowd without orders and were then joined by about fifty of their colleagues. They continued firing their high-velocity rifles, Sten guns and service revolvers long after the crowd had turned to flee in panic.

The massacre demonstrated the violence brought about by the apartheid system and marked the end of the period of peaceful protest that had been encouraged by Chief Albert Luthuli and the African National Congress (ANC). The South African government responded to demands for compensation by the families of those killed or maimed at Sharpeville by passing an Act (No. 61 of 1961) that protected the government and its officers against such claims. The Act, although passed after Sharpeville, was framed so that it came into effect retrospectively on March 21, 1960.

Above *Before the shooting at Sharpeville, an amiable, smiling crowd disperses. There are no threats to the police, no weapons visible. Yet seconds later, scores of people lay dead and wounded, shot by the police as they ran away.*

Those who had carried out the killings could not be prosecuted. No compensation would be paid.

Sharpeville did not mark an immediate turning point in South African history, but after the massacre fair-minded observers could doubt neither the evil of the apartheid system nor the inhuman lengths to which its adherents would go to defend it.

Twenty-five years later to the very day, a very similar massacre took place at Langa Township, near Uitenhage in the Eastern Cape. Twenty-one Black Africans were gunned down by the South African Police as they marched in a peaceful demonstration. As at Sharpeville, the victims were unarmed. The government response on this occasion was to relocate the township of Langa to a place more distant from the town center of Uitenhage (to which the Africans had been marching). Thousands of people were uprooted and placed in temporary tent accommodation as a result of the move. Many were unable to salvage their wooden homes from the onslaught of the bulldozer.

Below *Langa Township, Uitenhage. Blacks are ferried to the funerals of those shot dead by South African Police on the twenty-fifth anniversary of the Sharpeville massacre, March 21, 1985.*

Those who predicted disaster for the country following Sharpeville were confounded by the period of unprecedented prosperity for South Africa that actually occurred. Now, however, the birds of unjust repression are coming home to roost. The current crisis in South Africa has cost some 2,500 lives over a period of two and a half years and there is still no end in sight. The path that led to this crisis has been long and complex, but the Sharpeville massacre still stands as the outstanding flashpoint in South Africa's short and troubled history.

2
A divided land

The peoples of South Africa

South Africa is a multiracial and multicultural society. This undoubted strength has become a weakness because one minority group, the Whites, has specifically used racial discrimination as an instrument of government policy and as a means of maintaining its own position of privilege. For almost forty years, the official policy of the South African government has been to stress the differences between peoples in order to set them apart. The policy is called *apartheid*—literally "apartness."

In describing the peoples of South Africa, nearly every term that is used is politically loaded. The South African government officially recognizes four racial groups, which they now call Blacks, Whites, Coloreds and Asians.

Blacks are officially "persons who are, or are generally accepted as, members of any aboriginal race or tribe of

WHITES ONLY
TICKET OFFICE

STASIE MEESTER

Left *South African Railways, a bastion of apartheid, retains much "petty apartheid" including separate ticket offices for Whites and Blacks.*

Africa." For the most part they are Bantu-speaking peoples, but they also include the San-speakers (Bushmen) and Khoi-speakers (Hottentots). This group has been officially described in the past as "Bantu" and "Native." The term "African" is commonly used, but it is not officially accepted in South Africa because its use would imply that other groups are not African. There are about 22.5 million Blacks in South Africa, who make up about 74 percent of the population.

Whites are Caucasians who came originally from Europe and are commonly referred to as "Europeans." Those who are of mainly Dutch descent (about 60 percent of the Whites) prefer to be called "Afrikaners"—literally Africans, to stress that they belong to Africa, were born there and have nowhere else to go. There are over 4.5 million Whites in South Africa, forming only 15 percent of the population. Although only a small minority, they hold political power in the country and are widely distributed throughout South Africa.

Above *Market day in a city area inhabited by "Asians," who are mainly Indians and Chinese.*

"Coloreds" are people of mixed race, but they also include small ethnic minorities such as Malays. The Cape Coloreds are mainly the result of the unions between the Khoisan, White and Malay populations. There are over 2.6 million Coloreds in South Africa (8.5 percent of the population) and they are based largely in the western Cape Province.

"Asians" are mainly Indians, the descendents of those who came to the country from 1860 onward as contracted laborers to the Natal sugar plantations. Chinese people are officially Asians, but Malays who also come from Asia are not. The Japanese are classified as "honorary Whites." There are over 800,000 Asians in South Africa, less than 3 percent of the total population. They are heavily concentrated in Natal, mainly in the city of Durban.

Although racial segregation is so important in South Africa, there is no scientific basis for the racial classifications that are used. Instead, criteria of appearance and social acceptance are used. People are subjectively allocated to racial groups, and each year hundreds of people (690 in 1982–83) officially "change their race," which is a scientific impossibility.

3
A complex history

The history of South Africa is a complex fabric of inter-woven strands from many different cultural traditions. In terms of written records, it begins with the Portuguese voyages of discovery at the end of the fifteenth century, although these documents speak of a land that was already inhabited.

In 1487, Bartholomeu Dias rounded the Cape of Good Hope, seeking a sea route to India. At Kwaaihoek, some 500 miles (800 km) eastward, he erected a stone cross (*padrao*) before sailing home, confident that he had solved the problem of the route. Ten years later, Vasco da Gama completed the passage to India, arriving near Calicut in May 1498. It was left to the Dutch to establish a supply post for their East India ships at Cape Town, in 1652.

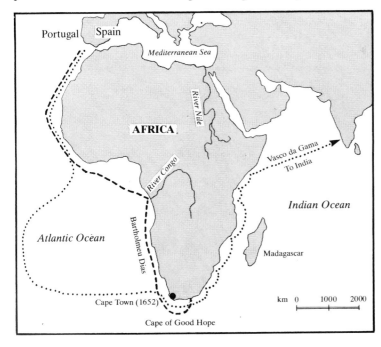

Left *This map shows the sea routes taken by Dias and da Gama in the fifteenth century. In 1652, the Dutch settled in Cape Town.*

15

Above *The Dutch governor of the Cape, Simon van der Stel, receives Hottentots (Khoi-Khoi) from Namaqualand who have brought with them pieces of copper from the "Copper Mountain." Van der Stel later visited the source of the copper in 1685.*

From 1658, free burghers (citizens) were permitted at the Cape and a permanent European settlement began. The economy was based on farming, and people were eager to acquire land. In turn, the sons of the Boers (farmers) all expected farms of their own. The Khoi-speaking peoples, who kept herds and flocks, and the San-speaking hunter-gatherers were together pushed aside, sometimes by land-purchase or conquest, often through decimation by European-introduced diseases such as measles and small-pox. Boer commandos hunted down the San because they hunted the Boers' cattle.

Within a century and a half, the Boers had reached the eastern Cape, over 375 miles (600 km) east of Cape Town. Here, in 1786, they established the small town of Graaff Reinet. However, they also encountered, for the first time, large groups of Bantu-speaking peoples moving westward toward them along the same strip of land between the coast and the Great Escarpment. Their economy was similar to that of the Boers and was equally land-hungry. The Bantu-speaking Africans were a much more formidable force than the Khoi-Khoi, not least in numbers. The first major clash, known to the Boers as the "First Kaffir War" and to the Africans as the "First War of Dispossession," was in 1779.

Into this situation the British came unwittingly in 1795 to protect the strategic sea route in the Revolutionary Wars. They restored the Cape, now constituted as the

Batavian Republic, to the Netherlands in 1803. However, some three years later, the British were back again not only to protect the sea route but also to face a deteriorating frontier situation.

British rule, and indeed that of the radical Batavian Republic, did not suit the frontier Boers. The British set up circuit courts and in 1807, they abolished the slave trade. They encouraged missionaries to work in the area who brought charges of murder and ill-treatment of slaves against several Boers. The accused Boers were tried before what they called the "Black Circuit" courts of 1812. The capital charges failed, but convictions were obtained on the lesser crimes of ill-treatment, which caused lasting disgruntlement among the Boers.

In 1815, many frontier Boers were further incensed following the Slaghter's Nek rebellion, which they considered had been caused and put down by harsh and insensitive measures. Khoi-speaking troops were used against the Boers, and clemency for those captured was refused. On one occasion when the gallows broke at an execution, six Boers were hanged a second time.

For the Boers, worse was to follow. The British were indecisive and inconsistent in their frontier policy. In 1820,

Below *In June 1803, Governor Janssens, representative of the Batavian Republic in the Cape, signs a treaty with the Xhosa Chief, Gaika, agreeing on the Fish River as a boundary between Black and White.*

Right *The trek-Boers took their ox-wagons through narrow passes in the Great Escarpment to reach the rolling plains of the South African high-veld, beyond the long arm of British colonial administration.*

5,000 British settlers were brought over to form a settlement that would act as a buffer between the Boers and the Xhosa, but the enterprise failed to stabilize the frontier. The abolition of slavery in 1833 took some frontier Boers to the edge of their patience. The amount and method of payment of compensation pushed them over. The Cape was awarded, by way of compensation, less than one-half the value placed on Cape slaves by the British themselves. Furthermore, the British government insisted that the compensation was payable only in London.

The Great Trek

The grievances held by the frontier Boers led 4,000 of them to undertake a trek away from the British yoke. The Great Trek extended the European frontier in Africa by over 930 miles (1,500 km). The trek crossed the Great Escarpment and the Orange River out of the Cape Colony into what one of the Boer leaders called a "strange and dangerous territory." It was far from unoccupied, as they had hoped. Its African population, just recovering from the shock waves of the Mfecane, tried to defend their land.

The Mfecane had its origin in the drought, famine and political instability that occurred in the corridor between the Drakensberg Mountains and the Indian Ocean in the 1820s. It involved mass migrations and widespread conflict, but also encouraged nation-building. Among the African nations forged at this time were the Zulu, the Basuto and the Ndebele.

On the high-veld, most resistance to the Boers came from the Ndebele, but the latter were finally defeated in 1837 and fled to the area that is now modern Zimbabwe. A Boer leader, Piet Retief, led a section of the trekkers into their

Below *On the high-veld, the Boers encountered resistance to their advance. They created defensive positions by hauling their high-sided wagons into a circle, or* laager. *Men and boys shot from the wagons while women and children reloaded the rifles in the comparative safety of the* laager *itself.*

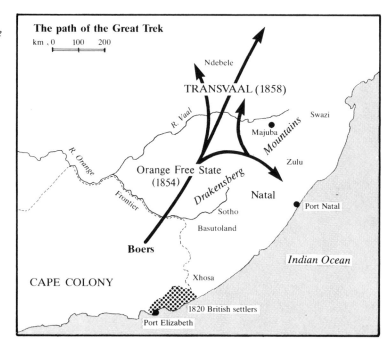

The path of the Great Trek

km 0   100   200

Ndebele

TRANSVAAL (1858)

R. Vaal

Swazi

Majuba

Mountains

R. Orange

Zulu

Orange Free State
(1854)

Drakensberg

Natal

Frontier

Sotho

Port Natal

Basutoland

Boers

Indian Ocean

CAPE COLONY

Xhosa

1820 British settlers

Port Elizabeth

land of milk and honey, Natal. Like Moses, Retief was not to enjoy its fruits, for he and 65 men were murdered by the Zulu king, Dingane, who then unleashed an attack on the Boer encampments and killed nearly 300 men, women and children. Boer vengeance came at Blood River on December 16, 1838, a day still celebrated by Afrikaners. Immediately afterward, the Boer Republic of Natalia was established.

The British came to Natal by sea and annexed Natalia in 1843, leading many Boers to trek away from British rule for a second time. The Boer republics of the Orange Free State (1854) and the Transvaal (1858) were recognized as independent, although the latter was briefly annexed by the British between 1877 and 1881 before they were defeated at Majuba. The Boers retained their independence until the second Anglo-Boer War at the end of the century. The Boers subjected the Africans within their republics, sometimes with British help. From an early date, some Africans were pushed to the outer areas of the republics, thereby creating reservoirs of cheap labor. The barren mountains of Lesotho, which like Basutoland came under British "protection and rule" in 1868, served such a function.

4
Diamonds and gold

In 1867, diamonds were discovered in the far interior of South Africa. The first alluvial diamonds were discovered in the beds of the Orange and Vaal rivers, and there was soon a "rush" of major proportions. The "dry diggings" (four "Kimberlite pipes," which were the source material of the diamonds) were discovered in 1870 within a span of nine months and within a radius of 2 miles (3 km) of what became the city of Kimberley. It was one of the greatest mineral discoveries of all time. It occurred in a South African interior that had until then produced only hides, wool and ivory. In addition, it was at this time that the overall importance of South Africa was about to be diminished by the opening of the Suez Canal in November 1869.

Below *Digging for diamonds in South Africa, in 1872.*

Kimberley quickly became the second city of South Africa. Diggers and speculators were attracted from all over the world, as were thousands of Africans too from the

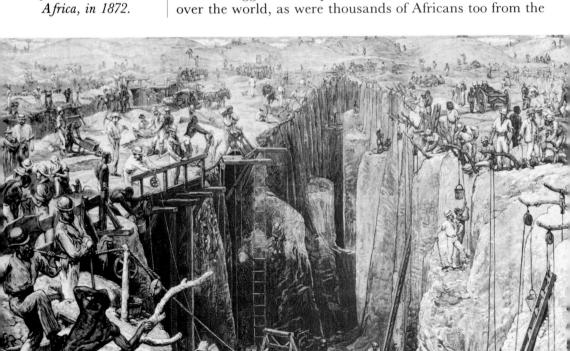

surrounding areas. In the early years, the new mines needed a great deal of manpower. By 1874, it was estimated that 25,000 Africans were employed at Kimberley. For the first time, large-scale paid employment was available to the African population, and with this first step in industrialization, the migrant labor system was born. As the mines became deeper, so the owners entered into mergers, and major capitalist groups grew up in time for the next major mineral discovery.

Kimberley lay between the Orange and Vaal rivers, north and east of where the rivers joined. Rights to the farms in this area had been granted by the Boer republic of the Orange Free State. Nevertheless, the British deviously backed a successful African claim to the area, so that it soon became part of the Cape Colony. As the British historian James Froude put it: "There was a notion that the finest diamond mine in the world should not be lost to the British Empire." The Boers were later paid a small sum of money in compensation, the equivalent of just one day's output from the mines.

In 1886, the South African interior amazingly yielded another mineral resource even richer than that at Kimberley, the gold of the Witwatersrand. The financial and technical resources at Kimberley were immediately

Above *The diamond town of Kimberley in the early 1870s, with the De Beers mine in the background.*

Above *Cecil John Rhodes made his money from diamonds at Kimberley and went on to have a country, Rhodesia (now Zimbabwe), named after him.*

Below *Prospectors on their way to the goldfields.*

employed to good effect in the development of the gold mines. The gold was located in minute quantities in massive quartz beds, which meant that the Rand (Witwatersrand) mines were from the first much more capital intensive and used a great deal of machinery. Towns sprang up all along the Rand, the chief among them being Johannesburg.

Kimberley and the Rand together created an unprecedented demand for labor that could not be met through normal market forces. This was because the mineowners wanted cheap labor, and African peasant agriculture was prosperous and independent. In 1894, Cecil Rhodes, the mining magnate who had become prime minister of the Cape Colony, passed the Glen Grey Act through the Cape parliament. Among other provisions, it imposed a poll tax on Africans, which forced them to undertake paid employment. This, of course, was mainly available at the mines. From 1893, the Rand mineowners set up labor-recruiting organizations to scour the subcontinent for cheap migrant labor, a system that prevails to this day, despite the social hardship it causes and its basic inefficiency.

Most of the capital used to develop the gold mines came from Britain, as did most of the skilled miners and mine managers. But the mines themselves were situated in the South African Republic (Transvaal), and too centrally located for the British to attempt to claim ownership

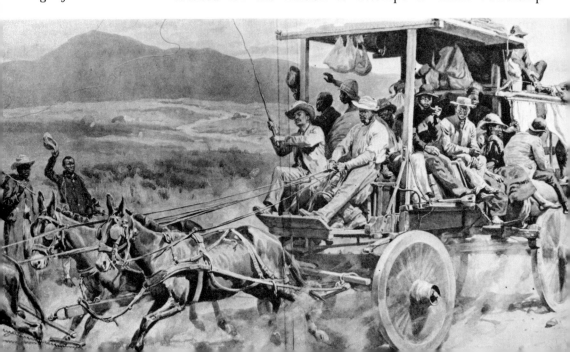

through a change in boundaries, as they had done at Kimberley. Other means of acquiring the mines were, however, soon devised. In December 1895, a military operation called the Jameson Raid was launched from the Bechuanaland border against Transvaal, which had long suspected that such an attack would take place. The plan was that the British on the Rand, the Uitlanders, supported by Jameson's force, were to rise in rebellion against Kruger's Transvaal government. The plan, however, fizzled out and there was no rebellion. Jameson and his men, whose approach was well known to the Boers, were forced to surrender after being shepherded into a well-prepared ambush. Jameson's patron, Cecil Rhodes, was forced to resign as prime minister of the Cape Colony, and the British government only narrowly avoided the stigma of being associated with the bungled plot.

Within four years the British were back, precipitating the Anglo-Boer War of 1899. Imperialism and capitalism marched hand in hand in a war of dreadful jingoism and ruthless tactics on the part of the British, which included a

Above *The Jameson Raid ended in ignominous defeat for Dr. Jameson and his men. They were forced to surrender by the Boers who had drawn them into a well-prepared ambush.*

Right *Man and boy with an ox-hide tent, part of a Boer commando at the siege of Ladysmith, 1900.*

scorched-earth policy and the use of concentration camps. The Boers put up a heroic defense and proved a harder nut to crack than had been anticipated. This was due in no small measure to their commandos, who fought a highly mobile guerrilla-type war. However, the war ended in defeat for the Boers with the Peace of Vereeniging, a treaty whereby the two Boer republics became British colonies.

The Union of South Africa
The British worked vigorously at postwar reconstruction. When the Liberals were returned to office, in 1905–6, they worked to unite the four South African colonies as the Union of South Africa. This was achieved in 1910, when South Africa emerged as the richest and most powerful state on the African continent. The British Liberals were eager to compensate for the wrongs of the Anglo-Boer War, which many of them had not supported. Consequently, they did not insist on changing the White-only franchise in the two former Boer republics, an omission many were later to regret.

One of the major issues facing the new Union government was that of African land. Over the years, the native Africans had been pushed back into land that was geographically and economically marginal. It was remote from railroad lines and other modern means of transportation

and communication, and it was of such poor quality that it could not support the population that had been crowded onto it. African land amounted to about 7.8 percent of the total area of South Africa, while Africans made up over two-thirds of the total population. General Hertzog was put in charge of the problem and asked to bring a Bill before

Below *Boer leader Louis Botha (with hunting crop) seated beside the British commander Lord Kitchener at the 1902 peace conference.*

Parliament in 1913. Unfortunately, he led the most nationalistic wing of the government and was often at loggerheads with the prime minister, Louis Botha, and his right-hand man General Smuts. Before this Land Bill was ready, Botha resigned simply in order to form a new administration that excluded Hertzog. A Natives' Land Act was duly passed in 1913, but it was in no way a permanent settlement of the land issue. It did prevent further encroachment by Whites, but it did not provide the additional land that was sorely needed by the Africans. The Act "scheduled" 22.5 million acres, or 7.3 percent of South Africa's total area, as African Reserves.

The government then appointed the Beaumont Commission to look into the problem. Its proposals, made in 1916, included increasing the amount of "Native Land" by releasing an additional 16.8 million acres to bring the total area to over 14 percent. The Commission also made the

Below *The Union of South Africa cabinet 1921, seated around the prime minister, General Smuts.*

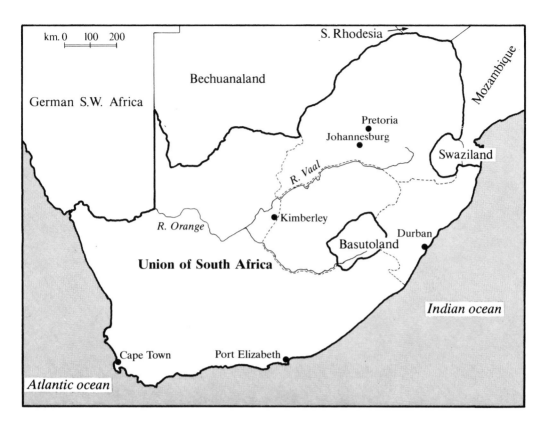

km. 0   100   200

German S.W. Africa

Bechuanaland

S. Rhodesia

Mozambique

Pretoria

Johannesburg

R. Vaal

Swaziland

R. Orange

Kimberley

Durban

Basutoland

Union of South Africa

Indian ocean

Cape Town   Port Elizabeth

Atlantic ocean

recommendation that the African lands be consolidated, in order to overcome the pressing problems of excessive fragmentation of their territory. The Beaumont proposals, however, were lost in Parliamentary Committee in 1917 and never became law.

A "permanent" solution had to wait until General Hertzog became prime minister. The Native Trust and Land Act of 1936 provided for African land to be expanded over a forty-year period by an additional "quota" of 15.3 million acres to 13.8 percent of South Africa, rather less generous than the Beaumont proposals. Incredibly, the target set in 1936 for the transfer of land to Africans has still not yet been reached, and the South African government has consistently regarded the 1936 legislation as the "final solution" of the land question. The total inadequacy of this solution, in the light of fifty years of rapid population growth and minimal investment in African land, is at the heart of the present-day problem of the African homelands.

Above *In 1910 the four South African colonies were united as the Union of South Africa, forming the richest, most powerful country in Africa.*

5
Industrialization and urbanization

From 1870, and particularly after 1886, South Africa could claim to have an industry-based economy. The industrial basis was mining, but there were also other industries that grew up specifically to service the mines and their machinery. However, it was not until 1924 that official steps were taken to encourage the growth of manufacturing industry in the Union.

In that year the "Pact" government, a coalition of Nationalists and Labor, was elected under Hertzog's leadership. This apparently unholy alliance betrayed the source of the electoral strength of the National Party, itself an alliance of "poor Whites," Afrikaners forced off the land largely as a result of the 1899–1902 conflict, and Afrikaner businessmen and intellectuals otherwise excluded from the Smuts-led Unionist coalition. The National Party has been consistently both populist and racist in its appeal to White

Right *Diamond sorters at Kimberley, at work on their felt-covered table.*

voters, offering them protection in the job market against the competition of Blacks.

The Pact government introduced legislation to encourage the growth of domestic industries to prevent the reliance on imports. Tariffs were imposed on finished manufactured goods, so that considerable savings could be made by importing parts and performing the final assembly in South Africa. The response was immediate, as foreign firms leapt to establish factories in South Africa in order to enjoy preference within the local market. One of the best examples of this is the automobile industry, which was among the first to respond by building factories in the country. Ford established an assembly plant at Port Elizabeth in 1924 and was followed by General Motors in the same city

31

Above *Rural South Africans were recruited for the mines from the late nineteenth century. The Glen Grey Act of 1894 forced many to leave the reserves for paid employment.*

in 1926. Both companies imported components in packs for local assembly. In time, their presence attracted manufacturers of other components, such as tires, glass and batteries, which are items readily left out of kits and with substantial local replacement markets. The industry grew rapidly as more and more component manufacturers built plants in South Africa in response to legislation that progressively rewarded local manufacture.

The comparative isolation of South Africa during World War II further encouraged domestic manufacturing, often using locally produced raw materials. By the 1950s, manufacturing was playing a very important part in the South African economy, making a contribution to the country's Gross Domestic Product that was in excess of that from mining.

The growth of manufacturing, based mainly in the large port cities and the southern Transvaal, led to a massive influx of people to these areas to provide the necessary labor. The towns found it difficult to cope with this rapid expansion in terms of the provision of housing and public services. As a result, there were widespread demands to control the influx and closely regulate the size of the Black urban population.

6
The National
Party in power

Although Britain had eventually won the Anglo-Boer War of 1899–1902, the peace undoubtedly belonged to the Boers, or Afrikaners. From 1910 to 1948, the Union of South Africa was led by three prime ministers, each of whom had served as a Boer general against the British. They were Louis Botha (1910–19), Jan Smuts (1919–24 and 1939–48) and Barry Hertzog (1924–39). Botha had taken the Union into World War I on the side of Britain, despite a rebellion among some Afrikaners. Smuts was the only non-Briton to serve in David Lloyd George's Imperial War Cabinet. Smuts also took South Africa into World War II on the British side, after narrowly winning a vote in the South African House of Assembly by 80 votes to 67. Again there was opposition, most significantly from the *Herenigde* (Purified) National Party led by a Cape *duminy* (clergyman), Dr. Daniel Malan. Many of Malan's colleagues were Nazi sympathizers and some spent part of the war in prison for undermining the South African war effort.

Smuts was better appreciated on the world stage, perhaps because he performed better there than he did in South Africa. He was a world statesman of considerable achievement who returned to South Africa to fight an election in 1948 at the age of 78. However, to everyone's surprise, he was beaten. Dr. Malan's National Party won 70 seats to the 65 of Smuts' United Party, thereby assuming a control that they have not since relinquished.

The National Party took time to consolidate its position and to work out an ideology beyond the simple concept of *baasskap* (control by Whites) with which it had entered power. It saw itself confronted with problems that went to the very heart of its main concern, the maintenance of

Above *General Louis Botha was Union prime minister from 1910 until his death in 1919.*

33

White supremacy in general and, in particular, the securing of Afrikaans domination.

Two premierships, Malan's and Strijdom's, were absorbed with these basic issues. When Strijdom died in office in 1958, he was succeeded by Hendrik Verwoerd, formerly Minister of Bantu Affairs. Verwoerd was armed with ideas that had been worked out during the 1950s. The economic prosperity of the 1960s, the Sharpeville massacre notwithstanding, provided the right climate in which these ideas could prosper.

Verwoerd's vision of apartheid covered the whole spectrum of South African life. For the "Native Reserves," the Tomlinson Commission Report of 1954 pointed the way from separate development to multinational development and from reserve to Bantustan, or "homeland." For the towns, the Group Areas Act of 1950 (subsequently amended many times) was to enforce strict residential segregation by race. Lines that were previously blurred were to be replaced by lines drawn finely, but very firmly. For industry, the color bar of job reservation was fiercely spelled out. In education, the "subversive" power of the missionaries was broken by the 1953 Bantu Education Act.

Right *Dr. Daniel Malan became South African prime minister in 1948 with a surprise victory over Smuts at the general elections.*

Left *Dr. H. F. Verwoerd, by training an academic psychologist, was the architect of apartheid. He became prime minister in 1958 and was assassinated in Cape Town in 1966.*

But the first aim of the Nationalists was to establish the Afrikaans cultural identity and their supremacy over English and other cultural groups. They had plotted for this through their secret society, the *Broederbond*, since 1915. Lapel pins proclaimed "the wonder of Afrikaans," a monument to the Afrikaans language was erected at Paarl, and the true spirit of Christian National Education was achieved through Afrikaans-speaking schools. The crowning glory was the establishment of the Republic of South Africa, which turned the defeat of 1902 into victory. The Republic was proclaimed, after a referendum among Whites only, on May 31, 1961. Verwoerd was prepared to forfeit membership of the British Commonwealth for this ideal and, having led South Africa out, returned home from London a national hero.

From Reserves to Homelands

The Tomlinson Commission (1951–54) recommended "separate development" as the only alternative to complete racial integration in South Africa. Under the Commission's proposals, the "Native Reserves" were to be divided into seven different ethnic "homelands," within which Africans were to be given increasing administrative autonomy. The economic development of the homelands was to be achieved by a combination of public and private investment in agriculture and industry. Targets were set for job creation to provide employment for Africans in their own areas. The fragmentation of the individual homelands was to be tackled by a program of consolidation that, although no additional land was to be allocated, would make them more viable. The full-scale development of the Bantu Areas was the initial step toward the practical realization of separate development.

What actually happened was significantly different. The Black population was divided among *ten* different homelands on the basis of cultural differences, except that the Xhosa people were divided into two homelands, the Transkei and the Ciskei. This lack of consistency, the small size of most of the homelands, and the fact that culture differences within the Black group were ignored, led to charges of "divide and rule."

The term "homelands" was itself emotive and misleading. The areas referred to were not, for the most part, traditional tribal heartlands. They were highly fragmented marginal areas into which the Africans had been pushed as a result of a steady expansion of White territories, which had been ultimately based on superior military strength. Only in the Transkei was there a large, single block of territory that was truly an African homeland.

Although eager to adopt the concept of separate development, the South African government consistently refused to meet the cost required to make the idea even remotely workable. The investment targets set by Tomlinson were never met. The improvement in African agriculture was never achieved. The non-agricultural job-creation program was not fulfilled because the government shied away from direct industrial investment in the homelands; the government preferred the development of "border industries." Under this policy, some industries in South Africa were to be re-sited, not in the homelands themselves but in the

Left *Xhosas in the Transkei homeland. The traditional pastoral economy is under pressure from overpopulation, overstocking and too little investment.*

37

Opposite *A map of the homelands (1985).*

Below *The grand design of apartheid separates people according to ethnic group. People who do not live among their own group are "resettled" in appropriate homelands, which are often barren, windswept places far from any paid work or other means of sustaining healthy life.*

adjacent White areas to which Black workers were to commute daily from within the homelands. Consolidation of the homelands was tackled without enthusiasm in contrast to the swift elimination of any "Black spots" in White areas, a process that contributed greatly to the misery of enforced African resettlement.

Administrative autonomy for each homeland was promoted, despite its obvious lack of credibility, because it was a way of evading the real issue by granting Black South Africans political "rights" outside White South Africa. Four homelands, the Transkei (1976), Bophuthatswana (1977), Venda (1979) and Ciskei (1981), were persuaded to take this bogus form of "independence." These territories are not recognized as separate states outside South Africa because the homelands are patently neither politically nor economically independent. All Black people in South Africa were seen as citizens of one or other ethnic homeland, where all their political rights were to reside. But the homeland electorates were not given the opportunity to vote for or against independence. In addition, the constitution and government of each small "state" is not

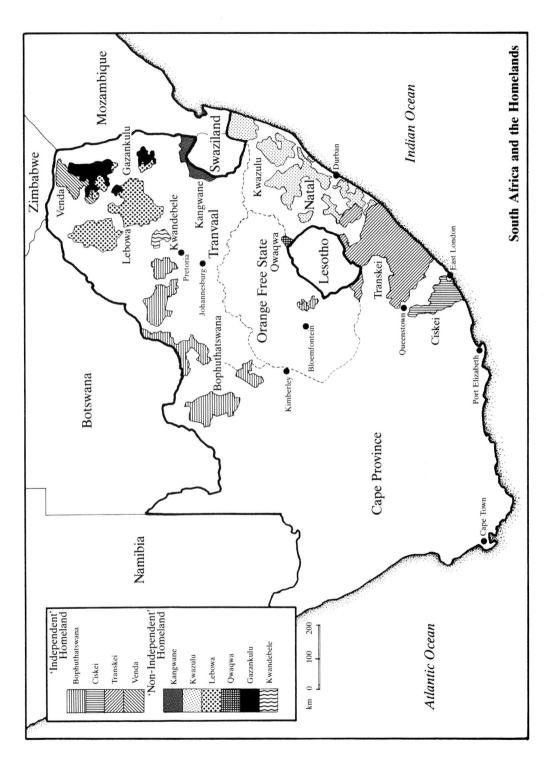

South Africa and the Homelands

Zimbabwe

Mozambique

Botswana

Namibia

Swaziland

Venda

Gazankulu

Lebowa

Kwandebele

Kangwane

Kwazulu

Natal

Kwazulu

Transvaal

Bophuthatswana

Orange Free State

Qwaqwa

Lesotho

Transkei

Ciskei

Cape Province

Indian Ocean

Atlantic Ocean

Durban

East London

Queenstown

Port Elizabeth

Bloemfontein

Kimberley

Johannesburg

Pretoria

Cape Town

'Independent' Homeland

Bophuthatswana

Ciskei

Transkei

Venda

'Non-Independent' Homeland

Kangwane

Kwazulu

Lebowa

Qwaqwa

Gazankulu

Kwandebele

km   0   100   200

democratic, with hereditary chiefs or nominated members holding a majority of seats in each legislature. Significantly, the largest group with a common language, the Zulu, have refused "independence." The Pretoria regime was further embarrassed in August 1986 when Kwandebele rejected "independence" at the eleventh hour following the assassination of its "puppet" leader.

The South African homelands are now poorer than ever. Between 1970 and 1980, their Gross Domestic Product per head of the population rose from 40 to 46 Rands, lower than any independent state in Africa. In addition, the rate of growth in the homelands is very low. Their agriculture is woefully inadequate to support populations that now greatly exceed Tomlinson's highest forecasts. Population densities in the homelands are among the highest in continental Africa, averaging 250 people per square mile in the non-independent homelands in 1980. Urban development is concentrated around the borders, where the homelands are adjacent to large White cities such as Durban and Pretoria. Consolidation proposals laid down in 1975 are not yet complete, and although government ministers protest that the 1936 land settlement may be exceeded (see page 29), the total allocation of land to Blacks is closely related to it. As a means of depriving Blacks of their South African citizenship and channeling their political aspirations elsewhere, the policy of creating homelands has failed. Separate development had only an outside chance of

Below *Refugees from the South African-encouraged civil war in Mozambique, in the homeland of Gazankulu.*

Left *A despised pass book, held by a resident of Tsakane Township near Johannesburg on the day in 1986 that President Botha announced the hated pass laws would be done away with.*

success. The unwillingness of the South African government to bear the considerable cost of their own ideological fantasy helped lead to its almost inevitable failure.

Urban South Africa

The development of industry in South Africa led to a massive influx of millions of Blacks into the towns from the countryside. The first line of defense against this mass migration was "influx control" by means of a series of pass laws. Every Black South African had to carry a pass book that was stamped by his employer. This book was proof of his right to urban residence. Hundreds of thousands of people were arrested each year for pass book offenses, and the pass books became emotive symbols of the apartheid state. It was a peaceful demonstration against this system that led to the Sharpeville massacre.

Once living within the urban areas, Blacks and other non-White groups found themselves strictly segregated.

Above *District Six, Cape Town: 40,000 people of mixed race were forced to leave this 225-acre area near the center of Cape Town by the South African government who had, against all protest, designated it for Whites only. A bulldozer waits to begin demolishing "colored" apartments under the heights of Table Mountain.*

The Group Areas Act laid out the basic rules for urban segregation by race. Blacks were permitted to live only in "townships" or "locations," which were laid out by the authorities and were situated usually on the outskirts of the "White" towns and cities. Coloreds and Asians, who had frequently occupied inner-city districts, found their districts reallocated to Whites. They were also forced to move to peripheral, often far-distant townships. The most notorious example of such a removal occurred in the mid-1970s in District Six in Cape Town, which had been occupied by Cape Coloreds literally for centuries, as well as by some Blacks and Whites. Despite protests from all cultural groups, the area (which lies adjacent to the Cape Town central business district) was bulldozed. The displaced people were relocated in remote townships, the most distant of which, Atlantis, is more than 28 miles (45 km) from the center of Cape Town.

The official townships are bleak and inhospitable. Row upon row of identical houses are separated by wide dirt roads, which, like the boulevards of Paris, owe their design to thoughts of crowd control. Unlike the Parisian boulevards, they are treeless, dusty, windswept tracts patrolled in times of urban unrest by the armored vehicles of the South African Police and Defense Force. The townships are fenced in and are set back from main roads by a regulated distance, so that if there are any problems they can be easily closed off without fear of disruption to "normal" life outside.

Houses in the townships are badly overcrowded and are poorly provided for, some lacking the most basic services. In the best-known townships region of all, Soweto (the SOuth WEstern TOwnships of Johannesburg), only about 10 percent of the homes have electricity. The provision of services within the townships is generally poor and residents are, in effect, forced to use city center services daily. The cost of travel to the city center is often very high, because the townships are deliberately placed in remote regions. The townships residents are the least able in the

Below *A bath for a baby in the townships where there is no running water or other basic facilities.*

Right *Black commuters perch between the carriages on the overcrowded trains that run from Black townships to White city centers.*

community to afford the very heavy costs involved in commuting and general transportation.

The official townships portray the more favorable face of urban living for the South African Blacks. Because urban building projects have failed to keep pace with population growth and the huge migration from rural to urban areas, many Blacks have to live in squatter camps and shanty towns. Here there are virtually no services (e.g. running water, lighting, heating, etc.) and the filth and squalor is awful. From time to time, these camps are bulldozed by the authorities, who often remove the residents to the African homelands. Here, these people have to live in bleak re-settlement camps, which hold few job opportunities.

The problem the government faces is that while urban Blacks are an economic necessity for the continued prosperity of White South Africa, they do not fit well into the concept of separate development. The attempt to make every Black, urban as well as rural, the citizen of a homeland has failed, and reform of the citizenship law is under way. The government has also relented and given Blacks the right to freehold ownership of land in the urban townships and, most significantly of all so far, has done away with the pass laws. But on the key issue of the Group Areas legislation, the government has refused to do anything except clutch at unreal concepts of city states for the Black townships—"like Luxembourg," according to the present state president, P. W. Botha. These ideas have yet to be fully spelled out.

Below *The tent town of Khayalitsha outside Cape Town, home for many refugees from the trouble-torn squatter camp of Crossroads.*

7
The wind of change

Harold Macmillan made his "winds of change" speech to the Cape Town House of Assembly six weeks before Sharpeville. For once his sense of timing was wrong. Events in the Congo and the disintegration of the Federation of Rhodesia and Nyasaland gave rise to fears in White South Africa that White rule was under threat. However, an effective "buffer zone" was erected along the line of the Zambezi River, which was to last for fifteen years. The zone had at its center White Rhodesia, but the real bastions against change in the south were the two Portuguese colonies of Angola and Mozambique, which lay on either side of the subcontinent.

In 1974, a successful revolution against the right-wing dictatorship in Portugal led directly to the independence of Angola and Mozambique. In Mozambique, the neo-Marxist liberation movement FRELIMO took undisputed power in June 1975. In Angola three organizations (the MPLA, FNLA and UNITA) disputed power, and a civil war began even before the Portuguese withdrew. Independence was delayed until November 1975, when an MPLA government was recognized in Luanda. However, the civil war still continues there today.

Right *Hendrik Verwoerd and Harold Macmillan meet at Cape Town on February 1, 1960. At the South African House of Assembly, Macmillan went on to make his famous "winds of change" speech.*

Left *The countries surrounding South Africa, known as the "front-line states," with the exception of Namibia, which comes under South African administration.*

Growing isolation

The immediate impact of these developments on South Africa was, ironically, to come from the relatively remote Angola. On October 23, 1975, South African forces invaded Angola. Their intention was to support UNITA, the guerrilla force led by Jonas Savimbi and backed by the United

Left *UNITA rebel troops, supported by South Africa, entering a village in Angola.*

47

States. They wished to install a "friendly" government in the capital, Luanda, rather than the leftist MPLA. In this way South Africa would protect its interests in neighboring Namibia, the Trust Territory held by South Africa in defiance of the United Nations. The South Africans quickly advanced up the Angolan coast, taking Mocamedes, Lobito and N'gunza. Cuban troops and Soviet arms were rushed to support Cuban units already "advising" the MPLA, and the South Africans were held at the Cuvo River, 250 miles (400 km) south of Luanda. The South African invasion was self-defeating. It justified the MPLA use of Cubans and it led many African states to recognize the MPLA as the Angolan government. It also helped the U.S. Congress to decide to force the Ford administration into withdrawing support for the UNITA forces. The South Africans retreated to near the Namibian border, where they have remained ever since. They still make occasional forays into Angola, allegedly in "pursuit" of SWAPO guerrillas, but often to back UNITA offensives.

Namibia, the former German colony of South West Africa, has been administered by South Africa since Generals Botha and Smuts invaded it in 1915. South African administration was confirmed in 1922 by the League of Nations, but when the United Nations was formed and inherited the League's Trust Territories, South Africa refused to recognize the United Nations mandate to decide on the administration of these areas. Legal disputes

Below *South African troops operate within southern Angola, penetrating for hundreds of miles in "hot pursuit" raids against SWAPO guerrillas.*

Left *Namibia, a U.N. Trust Territory, is still administered by South Africa in defiance of an International Court of Justice ruling. SWAPO is the primary liberation movement in Namibia but is not recognized by the South African government.*

raged for many years at the International Court at The Hague, which eventually ruled against South Africa's involvement in Namibia. The United Nations then demanded from South Africa a timetable for withdrawal from the country, but South Africa has successfully used delaying tactics and has tried to install "puppet" administrations, which have excluded the principal liberation movement, SWAPO. Namibia came close to independence in 1978, but the momentum was not maintained and the situation has been in stalemate since then.

Below *In April
1980, Zimbabwe
attained independence.
Here, the multiracial
cabinet of Robert
Mugabe is sworn in
in front of the
president, the Rev.
Canaan Banana.*

Independence for Mozambique had an immediate effect on White Rhodesia. The illegal regime of Ian Smith had its direct access route to the Indian Ocean cut off and a long border was opened up along which guerrilla attacks could be made. White rule faced an inevitable end. In April 1980, Rhodesia became independent under the leadership of Robert Mugabe and was renamed Zimbabwe. States with Black majority rule now surrounded South Africa and Namibia.

8
The cosmetic reform of apartheid

The long delayed "wind of change" had a profound effect on Blacks in South Africa. If Mozambique could have genuine independence with majority rule, then why not South Africa? The defeat of the South African Defense Force in Angola demonstrated the vulnerability of the White regime for the first time. Furthermore, the late 1970s was a time when the National Party was running out of ideological steam, and the rumblings of scandal within its own ranks began to contribute to a lack of certainty of direction for the apartheid state. These factors combined to contribute to a violent upheaval in the Black townships, which first erupted in Soweto in 1976.

Soweto: Afrikaans and the language of oppression

The immediate spark that caused the conflagration was the insistence of the government that Afrikaans should be the language used for teaching in Black township schools. Young Blacks quite reasonably looked upon Afrikaans as the language of oppression in South Africa. Furthermore, it did not enjoy the universal status and usefulness of English, or as one Soweto slogan put it: "Afrikaans is a tribal language." The insensitivity of Afrikaners to the language issue was extraordinary, especially when one recalls their own angry reaction to a crass attempt by the British to impose English on the Boers after their 1902 defeat.

The Soweto uprising was harshly dealt with. Many more people were killed on June 16, 1976 than at Sharpeville, most of them children. The consequent unrest spread throughout South Africa, and it was met with uncompromising violence, the final nationwide death toll being about 500. Unlike at the time of Sharpeville, television pictures were flashed around the world showing the

Above *The Soweto riots in 1976 erupted on the educational issue that Black South Africans would be taught in Afrikaans only, considered the language of oppression by Blacks. Here paramilitary police examine a body lying in the street.*

sickening violence perpetrated by the so-called forces of law and order. Although the unrest within the townships was eventually quelled, widespread resentment smoldered on. Many hundreds of schoolchildren left the country for guerrilla training with the ANC and the PAC. The South African government wavered, caught in a period of uncharacteristic uncertainty. Finally it opted for a major change of direction heralded by the setting up of a series of official Commissions.

Economic necessity had been nibbling away at the clean cut edges of apartheid for some time. Its more petty aspects (such as separate benches for Whites and Blacks in parks) were being steadily eroded. The external image of apartheid was already a matter of concern. A change of leadership brought to office P. W. Botha who, as former Defense Minister, had the close cooperation of the South African military. This change reinforced a feeling that some reform was not only desirable but could also be effectively contained.

The attempt at controlled change

In 1977, the South African government appointed two Commissions. They were referred to by the names of their respective chairmen, Riekert and Wiehahn, and they were formed to look into the "Utilization of Manpower" and "Labor Legislation." The move reflected the importance of the growing problem of the supply of labor in a period of economic structural change. There was a greater need for skilled labor, but it was in short supply largely because of the restrictive practices of apartheid itself. The collective strength of Black labor had been demonstrated in the early 1970s, when collective action began to be taken in Namibia and Natal.

Both Commissions reported in 1979. Wiehahn recommended that legal recognition should be extended to African trades unions and that the principle of statutory job reservation should be abolished. Riekert made several recommendations to the effect that the lot of the urban African should be improved. It, too, called for the abolition of job reservation and discussed influx control and the pass laws. The government cautiously accepted some recom-

Below *Trade Union recognition has led to the emergence of an increasingly strong Mineworkers Union. Issues include not only the question of safety in the mines, where the recent record is appalling, but also political matters—a development that alarms the South African government.*

mendations, but either modified or rejected most of them. For example, the principle of recognition for Black trade unions was accepted, but membership was restricted to those Africans in permanent work, thereby excluding migrant workers. But the true significance of these two Commissions was that they signaled change, albeit forced on the apartheid state through economic circumstances. What is more, the Commissions raised expectations of further change in the future. The monolith of apartheid was not just fraying at the edges, it was seen to be developing cracks.

The boldest move in this period of change also occurred in 1977, when constitutional reform was first suggested by the National Party. The spade work was done by the Schlebusch Commission, which reported in 1980. It recommended replacing the Senate with the President's Council, to which the burden for constitutional change passed in 1981. The Council reported in 1982 and the government tabled its own watered-down version of its proposals in 1983. These were duly passed after an incomplete debate in

the House of Assembly and later received a two-thirds majority in a referendum of White voters only.

The new constitution provided for an executive president, backed by a President's Council, and a system of government that had three houses representing the separate ethnic groups of Whites (House of Assembly), Coloreds (House of Representatives) and Indians (House of Delegates). Blacks were specifically excluded from these reforms and still had no political rights within South Africa outside the homelands. This exclusion of the Blacks from the political process led to fierce criticism of the new constitution, which was seen as an attempt by the National Party to turn the South African political struggle from one between White and Non-White to Black versus Non-Black. The ruling party in the House of Assembly is ensured a built-in majority of the members of the President's Council, and throughout the government system the balance is carefully weighted to guarantee White, and specifically National Party, supremacy. What was proclaimed as an exercise in power-sharing was in fact little more than a means of

Opposite
Sjambok *(rhino-hide whip) wheals on the back of a Black student, the result of a beating by Police in October 1985. His friend who was also beaten died as a result.*

Below *South African police with riot gear, dogs and* sjamboks *brutally break up a peaceful student demonstration in Johannesburg, May 30, 1986.*

providing a forum where members of ethnic minorities might air their views. This was how the overwhelming majority of Asians and Coloreds saw the situation, because fewer than 20 percent of them voted in the elections of 1984. What the elections actually brought was, beginning in September 1984, a wave of protest from the Black community at its continued exclusion from political representation. This unrest among the Black population led directly to the declaration of a "State of Emergency" and the current crisis in South Africa.

Again the Black townships were the focus of dissent and of brutal repression by the South African Police and Defense Force. Scenes thick with plastic bullets, tear gas, *sjamboks* and armored vehicles filled the world's television screens. Under the provisions of the State of Emergency, television cameras were banned because the government claimed that they incited acts of violence on the part of the Blacks. The death toll was heavy and actually rose after the ban on television coverage to an average of over four Blacks killed each day. Massacres by the security forces occurred at Queenstown, Mamelodi and, incredibly, on the twenty-fifth anniversary of the Sharpeville massacre, at Langa.

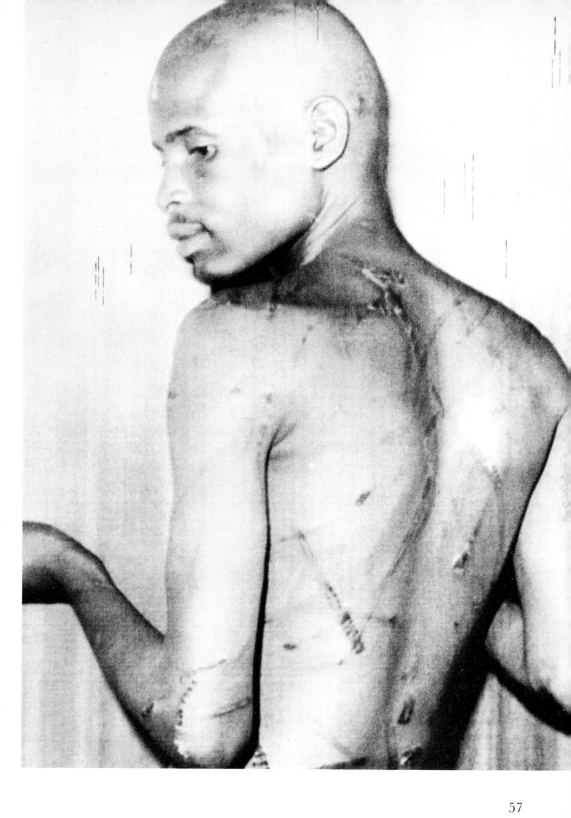

The turmoil continues, barely contained but not ended. A new, more stringent State of Emergency was imposed in May 1986 and the ban on television pictures was extended to include a massive campaign of press censorship by the end of the year. Naked authoritarianism was taking over in

Right *March 22, 1986 witnessed another mass funeral. Black youths carry the coffins of their comrades killed by the South African Police in township rioting. Funerals were used as opportunities for further political demonstration, a right now brutally repressed.*

an increasingly beleaguered South Africa. These first death throes of apartheid are not limited to South Africa, but embroil the whole of the subcontinent of southern Africa and bring a sense of shame, anger and exasperation to the Western world.

9
Dismantling apartheid

The present tragic state of affairs in South Africa owes much to the wind of change that brought majority rule to the rest of southern Africa. But the majority-ruled states of the subcontinent are relatively small and poor and are dominated by South Africa economically, politically and militarily. Among the ten states of southern Africa, South Africa has 20 percent of the land area, 40 percent of the population and 80 percent of the economic wealth. South Africa would like to maintain this domination, not least because its neighbors are political hostages. They can be placed in the firing line at the first threat of any external move to impose sanctions as a means of exerting pressure on the apartheid regime to accelerate change.

SADCC and the "constellation of states"
In 1979 President Botha put forward the concept of a "constellation of states" in Southern Africa, through which he sought to promote the virtues of regional cooperation. His neighbor states interpreted his ideas as a means of perpetuating their dependency on South Africa. Their reaction, in the same year, was to set up the South African Development Coordination Conference (SADCC), through which they hoped to pull away from the South African orbit toward truly independent economic and political development. The formal constellation idea has faded, but many of its aims are being achieved in an ad hoc manner by fair means and foul.

The key to the dependency of the SADCC countries on South Africa is the railroad and port network that is dominated by South Africa. Over half the external trade of the relevant SADCC countries is channeled through South Africa, and that proportion is likely to grow. South African railroads and harbors are well run and have spare capacity. Railroads in the SADCC states are badly run and are

poorly maintained while the ports are inefficient and congested. But many SADCC railroads are also out of action because of the activities of guerrilla groups in Angola and Mozambique that are heavily backed by South Africa. The Benguela railroad in Angola has been closed since 1975, thanks to the actions of UNITA. The Nacala railroad in

Above *Crowds celebrate Zimbabwe's independence, April 19, 1980.*

northern Mozambique has been closed since 1983 by MNR rebels, who have also shut down the Malawi to Beira railroad and the Chicualcuala line from Zimbabwe to Maputo. South Africa promised to withdraw its support of the MNR at the Nkomati Accord with Mozambique in 1984, but it has clearly failed to do so. The Zimbabwe to Beira line is kept open only by the Zimbabwean army, which protects the 200-mile (320-km) corridor across Mozambique from Mutare to the Indian Ocean.

The SADCC plans to overcome its dependency on South Africa. South Africa plans otherwise. In the short term, the main concern is that the poor countries of southern Africa are very much at the mercy of South Africa. The South African Foreign Minister, Pik Botha, has spelled out quite crudely that his government will see to it that any sanctions that are imposed against South Africa will hurt its neighbors first.

Sanctions and other Western measures
From September 1984 onward, Black unrest in the urban areas has been constant in South Africa and it has been violently repressed. The world has been revolted by the brutality of the actions of the South African authorities, as one horror story after another has been transmitted via the world's television screens. Although Blacks also perpetrated their own acts of violence, not least the "necklace murders" (tires filled with gasoline, placed around the victim's neck, then set on fire) of alleged collaborators with the South African authorities, it was clearly seen that the basic cause of violence in South Africa was the patently unjust apartheid system and the methods employed to uphold it. World leaders were urged to bring pressure on the South African regime to make reforms and accelerate change. The American administration's policy of "constructive engagement" came in for strong criticism because it was obviously having no impact. Its failure undermined the arguments mounted by the United States, Britain, West Germany and other right-wing Western governments, that the South African government could best be persuaded into meaningful change by friendly encouragement, rather than by punitive measures.

As the situation within South Africa has deteriorated, so the call for international sanctions has increased. The Commonwealth Prime Ministers' Conference of 1985 was

only diverted from taking significant immediate action by Britain's Margaret Thatcher, who suggested the setting up of an Eminent Persons' Group (EPG) of Commonwealth leaders to assess the South African situation. The EPG report, published in June 1986 after several visits to South Africa, was a damning indictment of the South African government, which was clearly shown to be completely unwilling to make real changes. To underline their attitude

Above *An anti-apartheid demonstration in London, England, 1984.*

Above *Members of the Eminent Persons' Group of Commonwealth leaders, set up in 1985 to promote dialogue between Black African leaders and Botha's government.*

to the EPG, the South Africans attacked three Commonwealth countries in southern Africa during the Group's last visit to South Africa in May 1986. Not deterred by this calculated insult, Prime Minister Thatcher then sent Sir Geoffrey Howe, her Foreign Secretary, on a fruitless and humiliating mission to try to negotiate with the South African government. Once again, they rudely demonstrated their utter contempt even for their friends in the West.

The outcome of these snubs to the West was the implementation of punitive sanctions against South Africa as agreed by the Commonwealth (although only minimally by Britain), together with less severe sanctions reluctantly imposed by the European Economic Community (EEC), and stronger measures exacted by the United States Congress, where both the House of Representatives and the Senate voted by more than a two-thirds majority to override Ronald Reagan's presidential veto. The way in which Western leaders have clung to means of supporting the apartheid regime has been hard for many people to condone. It has also served to polarize public opinion about the effectiveness of sanctions to the point at which reasoned discussion has become virtually impossible.

In the last three months of 1986, a new phase was opened in world action against apartheid when several large multinational companies began to close down their operations in South Africa. The American corporations of Coca Cola, Eastman-Kodak, General Motors, EXXON and IBM Computers have all withdrawn from the country, and in late November the British-based Barclays Bank pulled out. These withdrawals are not all as complete as they might seem because, as in the case of General Motors, the plant has been taken over by local management, who will continue to receive supplies of vehicle parts for local assembly from the parent company. The Eastman-Kodak pullout seems to be the most complete because there was no local takeover of the company as a going concern.

Below *In July 1986, Margaret Thatcher sent Sir Geoffrey Howe on a humiliating visit to Southern Africa. He received the friendliest greeting from President Samara Machel of Mozambique. Later in 1986 Machel tragically died in an air crash.*

Above *Part of an anti-apartheid demonstration in London 1985. This poster contributed to the withdrawal of Barclays Bank from South Africa in November 1986.*

The effect of this disinvestment on South Africa is likely to be more devastating for the country psychologically than economically. But it is also true that, for the first time in decades, South Africa is not seen as a place for investment. The Barclays' chairman emphasized that the decision of the Bank to pull out was taken largely on commercial grounds. More disinvestment would further undermine business confidence and would rapidly turn South Africa into an inward-looking, siege economy.

It is argued that as a combination of sanctions and disinvestment bites and the South African economy comes under greater pressure, so the capacity for peaceful change is diminished. Coupled with that is the fear that, when threatened, the Afrikaner will stubbornly resist all reasonable approaches. Against these arguments it must be said that all reasonable approaches, such as those of the EPG and Sir Geoffrey Howe, have already been rejected quite bluntly, blatantly and humiliatingly. Furthermore, the capacity for change is tied more to political will than to economic maneuverability.

Below *State President Botha at a march past in Johannesburg, November 1986.*

10
The future

Opposite *Death in police custody is the common fate of many South African protesters. The funeral of one victim, Andries Raditsela, who died on May 6, 1985, attracted 30,000 mourners determined to carry on the protest against their oppressors.*

What the future holds for South Africa is, in detail, impossible to predict. The balance of numbers is such that, in the long term, majority rule must prevail. Whites, who form a diminishing proportion of the population, and who already represent less than 15 percent of the total, cannot cling to exclusive power for ever. It is hoped that in the future power can be shared, so that minorities are not swamped by the majority. This implies a constitution of careful checks and balances and embedded safeguards. Experience elsewhere in Africa does not inspire confidence about this possibility. An ultra right-wing leader in South Africa, Dr. Andries Treurnicht, has declared that there is no such thing as power-sharing, and the young Blacks in the townships are likely to agree. If they are right, then a prolonged and very bloody struggle lies ahead.

Right *Extreme right-winger Eugene Terreblanche with supporters under the neo-Nazi emblem of his party, the Afrikaner Resistance Movement.*

STUBBORNESS BROU
REVOLUT
THE PEOPLE SH
OUR POWER IS D
WAR!
CRUSH APARTHEI
TH

Date chart

1487 Bartholomeu Dias rounds the Cape of Good Hope.

1498 Vasco da Gama reaches India via the Cape Sea Route.

1652 Dutch East India Company station established at the Cape.

1658 The first free burghers at the Cape.

1779 The first major clash between Boers and Bantu-speakers.

1795 First British occupation of the Cape.

1806 Second British occupation of the Cape.

1807 British abolish the slave trade.

1820 5,000 British settlers brought to the eastern Cape.

1833 British abolish slavery but pay compensation to Boers in London.

1836 The Great Trek begins.

1838 Retief murdered. Zulus defeated at Blood River.

1867 Diamonds first discovered near Hopetown on Orange River.

1870 "Dry diggings" discovered and Kimberley founded.

1886 Gold discovered on the Witwatersrand; Johannesburg founded.

1895 Jameson Raid on the Transvaal.

1899 Second Anglo-Boer War begins.

1902 War ends with Peace of Vereeniging.

1910 Union of South Africa formed as self-governing dominion.

1914 Louis Botha takes South Africa into World War I.

1924 Pact government of Nationalists and Labor under Hertzog. Tariff walls erected to encourage industrialization.

1936 Land Act passed by Hertzog's government.

1939 Smuts takes South Africa into World War II.

1948 National Party under Malan defeats Smuts' United Party

1950 Group Areas Act passed.

1954 Tomlinson Commission reports.

1958 Verwoerd succeeds Strijdom as prime minister.

1960 Sharpeville massacre. 67 Africans killed by police.

1961 Republic of South Africa established and leaves Commonwealth.

1966 Verwoerd assassinated. Succeeded by Vorster.

1976 Soweto disturbances put down with violence.

1976 Transkei homeland declared "independent."

1977 Riekert and Wiehahn Commissions set up. Bophuthatswana homeland declared "independent."

1978 P. W. Botha succeeds as state president.

1979 Venda homeland declared "independent."

1980 Schlebusch Commission set up.

1981 Ciskei homeland declared "independent."

1983 New Constitution passed after referendum among Whites only.

1984 Elections for Colored House of Representatives and Asian House of Delegates. Unrest begins in Black townships.

1985 State of Emergency. Massacre at Langa. 21 Africans killed.

1986 Commonwealth Eminent Persons' Group visits South Africa. Commonwealth votes for sanctions against South Africa. Britain and the EEC impose limited sanctions. United States Congress overrules President Reagan to impose sanctions against South Africa. Barclays Bank, Coca-Cola, Eastman-Kodak, General Motors, IBM Computers disinvest from South Africa.

1987 The National Party returned to power. Voting showed a swing to the Right.

Glossary

Afrikaners Descendants of the original Dutch settlers, augmented by French Huguenot and other European strains. In general they speak Afrikaans, belong to the Calvinistic Dutch Reformed Church and make up about 60 percent of the White population of South Africa. They form less than 10 percent of the total population.

ANC African National Congress. South Africa's oldest political party, founded in 1911. Banned by the South African government, the ANC has a "government-in-exile" based at Lusaka, Zambia. The president is Oliver Tambo whose former colleague, Nelson Mandela, has been in a South African jail for twenty-five years.

Apartheid Literally "apartness." Used to describe the racial segregation policies of the National Party in South Africa since it came to power in 1948.

Asians Mainly Indians, descendants of people who came as indentured laborers to the Natal sugar plantations from 1860. Also includes Chinese, but not Malays who are officially Colored or Japanese who are "honorary Whites."

Batavian Republic The Dutch Republic to which the Cape was passed by the British in 1803, until it was reconquered by Britain in January 1806.

Blacks "Persons who are, or are generally accepted as, members of any aboriginal race or tribe of Africa." Mainly Bantu-speaking people, but also including San-speaking and Khoi-speaking groups. Also referred to as Africans and formerly in South Africa as "Natives" and "Bantu."

Boers Literally "farmers" (from the Dutch). Used more widely to describe the people of mainly Dutch descent who are now known as Afrikaners. "Boer" is still used, but in a rather derogatory way when referring to Afrikaners.

Broederbond Literally "brotherhood." Secret society founded in 1915 to work for Afrikaner supremacy within South African White society.

Coloreds People of mixed race, Cape Coloreds, Griquas and also members of ethnic minorities such as Malays.

Disinvestment Removing assets or money invested in a country. This sometimes involves factory closures.

Great Trek A series of migratory movements by about 4,000 frontier Boers away from British rule in the Cape Colony 1836–38.

FRELIMO *Frente de Libertacao de Mocambique,* which came to power in Mozambique at the end of Portuguese rule in 1975.

Gross Domestic Product The annual total value of goods produced and services provided in a country.

Group areas Racially segregated zones in towns and cities for residential and commercial purposes for White, Colored and Asian groups.

Homelands An official apartheid term for what were previously known as "Bantustans" or earlier as "Native Reserves." Now official South African parlance favors "National States."

Khoi-Khoi Khoi-speaking pastoralists, formerly known as Hottentots, first encountered by Europeans in the Cape.

Laager A defensive formation of ox-drawn wagons used by the Boers during the nineteenth century against attack from African armies. Term now used to refer to coming together of Afrikaners to defend against any outside attack.

Migrant labor Persons who live in homelands or outside South Africa but work in "White South Africa" usually under contract. They enjoy no political rights at their places of work.

MNR Mozambique National Resistance. Guerrilla force set up by White Rhodesia to fight FRELIMO government in Mozambique. Now financed by South Africa and dedicated to the same aims.

MPLA *Movimento Popular de Libertacao de Angola.* Liberation movement that came to power in Angola at the end of Portuguese rule in 1975.

Pass Officially a "Reference Book" that had to be carried by all Blacks and produced on demand by the police.

Poll tax A tax levied on every person.

San San-speaking people, formerly known as Bushmen. Stone-age hunters and gatherers now confined to the Kalahari desert.

Siege economy An economy cut off from the rest of the world, which has to supply its own needs.

Sjambok Rhino-hide whip, now used by South African police in crowd control.

SWAPO South West Africa People's Organization is the main liberation organization in Namibia with headquarters in Lusaka, Zambia.

Transvaal A Boer Republic 1858–1902, known as the South African Republic. Annexed by the British 1877–81. Invaded by the British during the Anglo-Boer War of 1899–1902, when it became the Transvaal Colony, and in 1910 a province of the Union of South Africa.

UNITA *Uniao Nacional para a Independencia Total de Angola* Liberation organization that lost out to the MPLA in Angola in 1975, but has continued fighting a civil war ever since with South African support.

Picture Acknowledgments

The publishers would like to thank the following for the loan of their photographs in this book: BBC Hulton Picture Library 22, 24, 33; Camera Press 9, 13, 24, 26, 27, 34, 35, 46; Format Photographers 66; Mary Evans Picture Library 25; Network Photographers Frontispiece, 38, 40, 45, 63, 67; Peter Newark's Historical Pictures 18, 19, 21; Popperfoto 8, 10, 30, 31, 36, 41, 44, 48, 50, 52, 54, 56, 57, 61, 64, 65, 68, 69; Rex Features COVER; Topham Picture Library 11, 16, 17, 23, 31, 32, 47, 49, 53; Wayland Picture Library 12, 14. Maps are by Malcolm Walker.

Index